WEATHER & SEASONS

By
William Anthony

BookLife
PUBLISHING

ISBN: 978-1-78637-851-4

©2019
BookLife Publishing Ltd.
King's Lynn
Norfolk PE30 4LS

Written by:
William Anthony

Edited by:
Madeline Tyler

Designed by:
Gareth Liddington

Photocredits:

5 - Regina F. Silva, curiosity, uiliaaa, Martial Red, aShatilov, 8 - Artsem Vysotski, 9 - JIMMOYHT, Amanita Silvicora, 10 - avian, 12 - avian, 14 - intararit, 16 - Katerina Pereverzeva, 18 - Graphics RF, 19 - NotionPic, Sunny_nsk, 20 - Valeri Hadeev, Renee's illustrations, 21 - BigMouse, matrioshka, Tarikdiz, 22 - BreezyVector, Rvector, Vectors Bang, 23 - MSSA, Javid Kheyrabadi, Maike Hildebrandt.

Images are courtesy of Shutterstock.com. With thanks to Getty Images, Thinkstock Photo and iStockphoto.

All facts, statistics, web addresses and URLs in this book were verified as valid and accurate at time of writing. No responsibility for any changes to external websites or references can be accepted by either the author or publisher.

CONTENTS

Page 4   Weather
Page 6   Seasons
Page 8   Temperature
Page 10   Sunshine
Page 12   Clouds and Wind
Page 14   Rain and Floods
Page 16   Snow
Page 18   Thunder and Lightning
Page 20   Animals
Page 22   Extreme Weather
Page 24   Glossary and Index

Words that look like <u>this</u> can be found in the glossary on page 24.

WEATHER

Weather is what you can see in the sky and feel in the air outside. There are lots of types of weather. Some are:

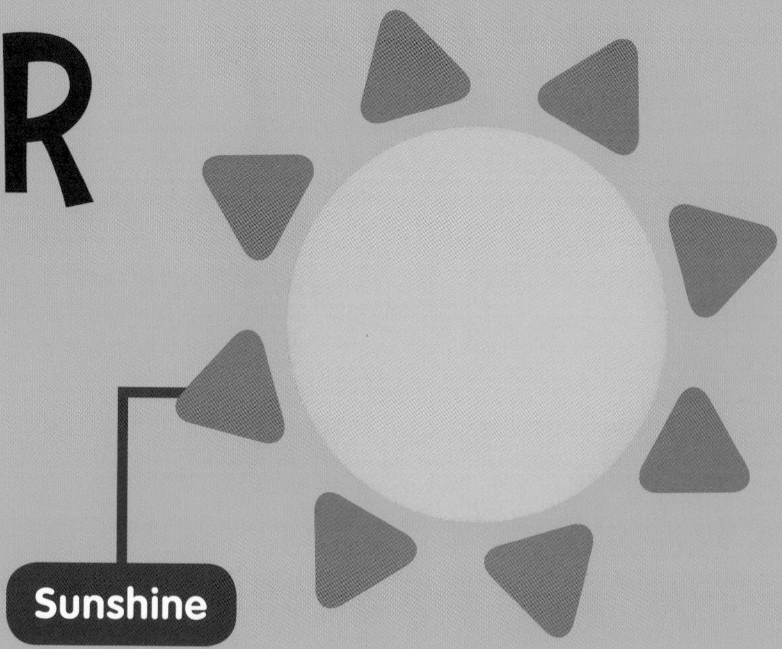

Sunshine

Rain

Snow

Wind and clouds

Humans can <u>adapt</u> to live in the most <u>extreme</u> weather <u>conditions</u>.

Different foods grow better in different types of weather.

Bananas grow best in hot weather.

Spinach grows best in cold weather.

5

SEASONS

There are four seasons and each one has different weather.
Summer is the hottest season with the most sunshine.
Winter is the coldest season and it might even snow.

Spring

Summer

Autumn

Winter

Earth moves around the Sun. At different times of the year, some parts of Earth are closer to the Sun than others. This creates the seasons.

During December in the UK, it is winter.

During December in Australia, it is summer.

TEMPERATURE

Temperature is how hot or cold something is.
Different seasons have different temperatures.

Water <u>freezes</u> at 0
degrees Celsius. Lakes
and rivers can freeze
in very cold winters.

The hottest place on Earth is Death Valley in the US. The <u>average</u> summer temperature is around 47 degrees Celsius.

The coldest place on Earth is Antarctica. The temperature can drop to almost -100 degrees Celsius. Brrr!

9

SUNSHINE

Earth spins as it moves around the Sun. Day is when your part of the planet is facing the Sun. Night is when you are facing away from it.

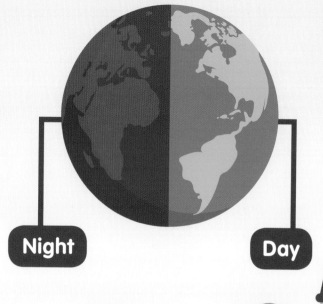

Night   Day

Yuma, Arizona, gets around 11 hours of sunshine every day. It is one of the sunniest places on Earth!

It takes around eight minutes for sunlight to reach Earth.

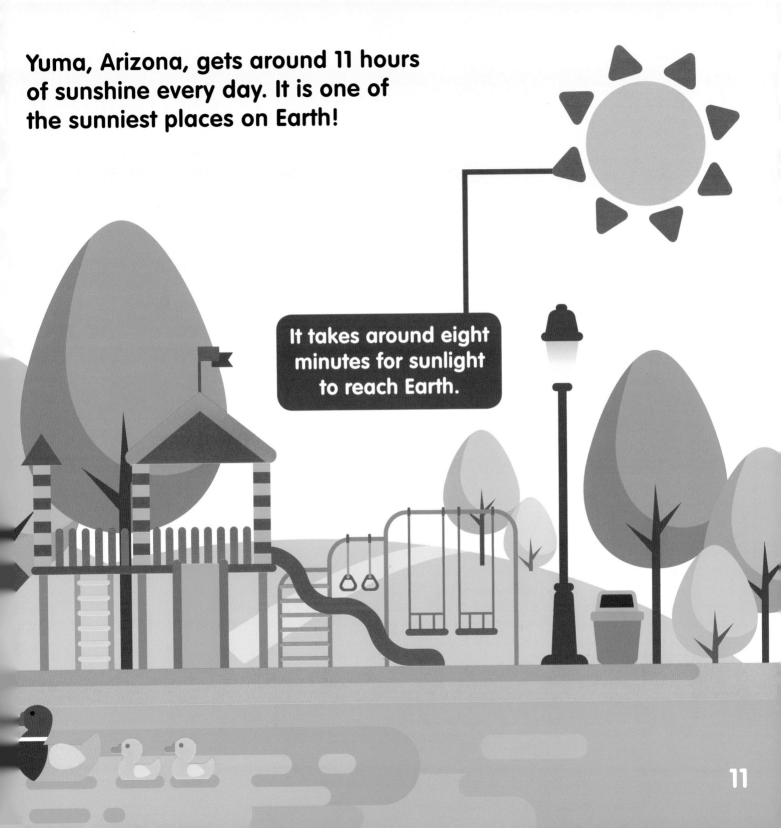

CLOUDS AND WIND

Clouds are the white parts of the sky. They are made when warm air on the ground rises into the sky and gets colder.

When the warm air rises, colder air rushes in to fill the gap it left. This rushing air is wind.

Some clouds can look big and fluffy. Others can look long and streaky.

Fog is a type of cloud that is found very close to the ground.

13

RAIN AND FLOODS

Clouds are made up of lots of tiny water droplets. When the droplets become too heavy, they fall from the sky back down to the ground. The falling water is rain.

When lots of rain falls over a short period of time, it can cause a flood. A flood is when an area of dry land gets <u>submerged</u>.

Floods can be dangerous. They can damage buildings and hurt people.

SNOW

Water freezes at 0 degrees Celsius, so when the sky gets colder than that, the water droplets in clouds freeze. When they fall from the sky, we get snow.

No two snowflakes look the same.

When lots of falling snow is mixed with a lot of wind, it is called a blizzard.

When the temperature rises above 0 degrees Celsius, snow will <u>melt</u>.

THUNDER AND LIGHTNING

A thunderstorm is a type of weather known for its flashes of light and booming sounds that come from dark clouds. The flashes are called lightning and the sounds are called thunder.

We see lightning before we hear the thunder it causes. This is because light travels faster than sound.

The sound of thunder travels around ten times faster than a cheetah.

ANIMALS

Animals are adapted to suit the weather where they live. Adaptations help animals to survive.

Meerkats have dark circles around their eyes that act like sunglasses. They live in bright and sunny Africa, so this helps them to see.

EXTREME WEATHER

The winds in the strongest <u>tornadoes</u> can spin at over 300 kilometres per hour.

The largest recorded hailstone to ever fall was almost the size of a volleyball.

Droughts are long periods of time with no rain. They can cause <u>crops</u> to die, which leaves some people with little food.

Thunderstorms are usually around 24 kilometres wide.

GLOSSARY

adapt   change over time to suit the environment

average   the typical and usual; not outside the ordinary

conditions   the state of the environment, such as the temperature, rainfall and food available

crops   plants that are grown on a large scale to be eaten or used

extreme   much beyond what is usual or expected

freezes   hardens into ice or becomes hard from cold temperatures

melt   to go runny like water, because of warm temperatures

submerged   covered completely by water

tornadoes   storms with strong winds that swirl down from the clouds to the ground in a funnel shape

INDEX

clouds 4, 12–14, 16, 19
cold 5–6, 8–9, 12, 16, 21
Earth 7, 9, 11
food 5, 23
hot 5–6, 8–9, 12, 21

humans 5, 15
light 11, 18–19
sound 18–19
Sun 4, 6–7, 10–11, 20
water 8, 14–16